Near Death

What You See Before You Die

2nd Edition

Table of Contents

Introduction

Thank you for purchasing the 2nd edition of *"Near Death: What You See Before You Die."*

If you're an ardent fan of the TV show, *1,000 Ways to Die*, you know that death is random, shows no favor, is always around, and can strike at any moment. You could be at your favorite restaurant on a date, gnawing on the complimentary fingerlings, sipping expensive chardonnay, immensely enthralled by the conversation, enjoying yourself as you await the main course.

Next, your date tells you a dirty joke. As you try not to laugh-out-loud, you make an attempt at holding in a burst of hearty laughter, as you take a sip of the expensive chardonnay, ordered to impress. And as it goes down your windpipe, the next thing you know is that it chokes the life out of you.

Before you breathe your last breath, you see flashes of light and watch as your *spiritual* body vacates your *physical* body. You look around the room and focus on the face of your date, filled with distress. You hear your date screaming out in fits of emotional agony as everyone miles around trying to resuscitate you. In that instance, you experience the urge to scream, "Don't cry! I'm right here," but before you do, a brilliant white light appears and magnetically beckons you. You want to get back into your body, get back to reality, and console your date, but the light becomes too intoxicating. Your senses have been overpowered, and in that moment, nothing matters more than moving towards the light. As you walk through the light, you experience a deep sense of elation, and just then, before you come out on the other end of the light, everything goes dark.

You wake up at the intensive care unit of your local hospital five days later. You are uncertain about a number of things: where you were, how you got here, and what happened. The only thing you know for sure is that you experienced something not from this world.

Every day, thousands of people around the globe experience something close to the experience described in the narrative above. These experiences are called Near Death Experiences (NDEs). Two humanly things are certain: life and death. What lives, must die; it's that simple. But not everyone on the brink of death actually dies. The lucky few "see the light" and live to tell tales of the other world, and that world that is far more real than our conscious world.

You're reading this book because death intrigues you. As a member of the living, you feel entitled to answers about death, but are left with only questions. *What is death? What does it feel like to die? Can I see, taste, smell, and feel death? Is there life after death? If so, what awaits us on the other side?"*

In this book, you will get answers. You will walk alongside real people who have had NDEs, and look through their eyes as they confront death. You will understand what awaits us on the other end. You will see what they have seen, and you will live to tell their stories.

NDEs – Deciphering the Truth

Background

As the name suggests, a near death experience (NDE) is any experience that may bring you or anyone else to the verge of death. An NDE is catching a glimpse of what happens to our soul or consciousness when we're on the brink of death, experiencing another world. It is living to tell the stories of angels, overwhelming heavenly love and elation from reuniting with loved ones.

NDEs have different associated aspects. This is because each of us has a different expectation of what awaits us on the other side of conscious life. As such, those who have experienced near death experiences often experience different things.

From real life accounts, a typical NDE, as described by those who experience it, may manifest in the form of an out-of-body experience or detachment from the body, warmth, levitation or feeling of levitation, dissolution, or the presence of a bright light. A person experiencing such an NDE typically has a strong uncontrolled desire to move towards the bright light, an eruption of joy, and serenity or inner peace.

Although they sound mystical, and do indeed have a barrage of mystery attached to them, NDEs are common occurrences, with approximately 9.57 million Americans reporting an NDE at some point in their lives.

NDEs and human fascination with death and what happens after conscious life is not a new phenomenon or something unique to the United States. NDEs transcend the boundaries of time, culture, and religious persuasion. NDE accounts were ubiquitous as far back as ancient Greece. The Christian Holy Bible is rife with accounts of NDEs[1], including the story of Elijah[2] and his ascension to heaven. Ancient books such as the Koran[3] and the Tibetan Book of the Dead[4] also contain references to NDEs.

---

[1] http://www.near-death.com/religion/bible/ndes-are-biblical.html

[2] https://www.biblegateway.com/passage/?search=2+Kings+2

[3] http://www.near-death.com/religion/islam.html

[4] http://www.near-death.com/religion/buddhism/afterlife-beliefs.html

The most prominent reference to NDEs in modern literature, and considered by some to be the first genuine, written account of an NDE, can be traced back to ancient Greece. In *The Republic*, Plato integrates three elements as part of the NDE philosophy in his story of Er: (1) the departure of the soul from the body and the presence of bright light (the light of truth), (2) the elevation of the soul to another plane that is profound and celestial, and (3) the memory of a vision of light and feelings of elation. Plato's three-part framework has shaped how we view and comprehend NDEs today.

Departure of the Soul from the Body

In a typical NDE, our celestial body (the soul) vacates our physical (corporeal) body and transports into the *afterlife*, a blissful and loving dimension that is in every way better than our current reality. The afterlife is as close as it gets to basking in the "garden-of-life" story most of us envision in our minds. Earlier on, we mentioned that NDEs are not as mystical as most of us envision them to be. Indeed, research[5] confirms that most phenomena associated with NDEs can be explained using biology. These explanatory models are present in categories such as physiology, psychology, and transcendental explanations.

While NDEs are different and often times manifest differently (NDEs often have different characteristics[6] and appear real to experiencers), neuroscience suggests an NDE is simply a hallucinatory state caused by psychological and physiological factors such as one's expectations of life after death or the nature of our transit from this life to the next.

Science has shown and proven that the 'feeling of being dead' is not synonymous with NDEs. Patients suffering from walking corpse syndrome also known as Cotard also strongly believe or experience delusion of 'being dead'. Medical science has also shown that this condition, i.e., the walking corpse syndrome, is especially manifest after immense trauma such as multiple sclerosis and many other traumas that affect the prefrontal cortex and the parietal cortex. The parietal cortex is involved in the attentional process while the prefrontal cortex is often involved in delusions.

OBEs – Elevation of the Soul

[5] http://www.sciencedirect.com/science/article/pii/S1364661311001550

[6] https://en.wikipedia.org/wiki/Near-death_experience#Characteristics

Another aspect of NDEs, the "out-of-body-experience" (OBE), has also been scientifically explained. Scientists interested in NDEs have associated OBEs with interrupted sleep patterns that come before sleeping or waking. A good example of this is sleep paralysis where you may feel paralyzed but remain aware of the outside world. OBEs are so common, in fact, that about 40% of the human populace has experienced an OBE at some point in their lives. Sleep paralysis is associated with vivid hallucinations that often result in the feeling of being outside one's body. Further, scientists have also discovered that out-of-body experiences can be triggered by stimulating the right temporoparietal junction in the brain.

Other NDE manifestations, such as communicating with or seeing deceased loved ones, are also scientifically explainable, and a common NDE feature. Visions of ghosts are manifest in patients suffering from Parkinson's disease with some of these patients proclaiming to have seen monsters. One Parkinson's patient presented with an abnormal functioning of dopamine, a neurotransmitter known to evoke vivid hallucinations.

Studies have also proven that the euphoria and out-of-body experience common in NDEs can also be triggered manually by administering recreational drugs such as *anesthetic ketamine*. The drug affects the brain opioid system, a system active in animals when they're under threat and can cause OBEs and vivid hallucinations.

The Bright Light

Another common aspect of NDEs that may not have a firm foundation in science is the aspect of moving through a tunnel, or towards a bright light. While this phenomenon has not been scientifically explained, scientists proclaim that tunnel vision normally occurs when there's a depletion of blood and oxygen flow to the eyes. Both of these symptoms are consistent with death.

The existence of a scientific explanation does not eliminate the possibility of a supernatural explanation. While scientists are quick to explain away NDEs as hallucinatory events triggered by the brain, rarely do scientists accuse NDE experiencers of promoting false accounts.

Having reviewed at a few explanations of some common NDE features, before we move on to real life accounts of what various people have seen while on these "other-worldly" escapades, let's begin with some common NDE characteristics, and then look at real-life accounts of each of these characteristics as explained by experiencers.

Characteristics and Features

As indicated earlier, NDEs manifest differently between individuals. Below is a list of traits common to most NDEs.

- The awareness of being dead or a sense of being dead

- An immense sense of peace, positive emotions, painlessness, and being removed from the world

- The "OBE perception" (outside the body feeling): Some NDE experiencers recall seeing, and being aware of, their surroundings in the moment. Others say they have "floated" from their corporeal body and seeing themselves being resuscitated

- The "tunnel experience": experiencers claim to enter a tunnel of darkness and experience a sense of moving up through a staircase or passageway

- An overpowering feeling of unconditional acceptance and unconditional love (often described as "heavenly or Godly love")

- Movement towards a brilliant white light or an abrupt immersion in an immense light. These accounts reference conversations with a "being of lights" or a deceased loved one.

- "Life is flashing before my eyes": where the experiencer receives an instantaneous life review

- Illumination into the nature of the universe and life - often followed by one's decision to return to the physical body. This manifests in the form of a border crossed by the experiencer. Experiencers often times explain their reluctance to return to the physical world.

- Sudden awareness of being in one's physical body.

Even though science contends that NDEs are merely psychological and physiological body and brain reactions, none of the scientists and researchers involved in the study of NDEs has ever disproven the supernatural elements claimed by experiencers.

Dr. Steven Laureys, head of the Coma Science Group at the university hospital in the city of Liege, Belgium highlights the contrast between the NDE and its natural world comparators. According to the memory characteristic questionnaire administered by Dr. Laureys, which tests for emotional and sensory recollection to measure how "real" and "intense" a memory is, *NDEs are extremely vivid compared to other memories, and are more than simple memories or hallucinations.*

In the memory characteristic test, Dr. Laureys and his team of researchers compared NDEs to other intense memories of monumental life events, such as births and marriages, as well as unconscious thoughts and dreams that did not occur in the physical reality. The researchers concluded that a real and recent memory is "richer" than a false memory, and that NDEs yielded results that were not only richer than imagined events, but real events as well. While Dr. Laureys' discovery with respect to the substantial contrasts between NDEs and false recollections was sufficiently compelling, he reached a far more profound conclusion when he varied the temporal components of NDEs and genuine memories. According to one of the conclusions in Dr. Laureys' study, *even where an experiencer's NDE occurred in the distant past, the experiencer's memory of the NDE was significantly more vivid and richer than the experiencers' true and more recent memories.*[7]

[7] http://www.cnn.com/2013/04/09/health/belgium-near-death-experiences/

NDE Accounts – Crystal McVea

What if you caught a glimpse of heaven's pearly gates, came face-to-face with God, and lived to tell about it?

Crystal McVea did. McVea, an Oklahoma schoolteacher, explains in her own words, "the only reason I'm alive today is so that I can proclaim the existence of heaven and God and tell others what awaits them on the other side."

McVea's NDE occurred in 2009 after a routine pancreatitis treatment went horribly wrong and she experienced an unexpected negative reaction to prescribed pain medication. Minutes later, McVea stopped breathing. She *felt* her heart stop. She *heard* her mother scream for help, and the nurses shout, *"Code Blue! Code Blue!"* She *saw* the nurses perform CPR on her lifeless body. She *tasted* and *smelled* oxygen being pumped into her lungs. The nurses' efforts to revive her weren't working, and McVea knew it.

McVea next recalls closing her eyes and drifting into unconsciousness for an extended period of time. What she didn't know at that time is that she was unconscious for nine minutes.

With her eyes closed and unconsciousness subsuming her, McVea recounts escaping the surrounding pandemonium opening her eyes to another realm: Heaven. In her OBE, she saw the tunnel and light, as well as magical beings, which she believes were angels.

McVea also reports another surreal vision: a gate. McVea's gate was white, rich with spherical, "pearl-like" apparatuses. She believes the gate was an entrance into Heaven.

McVea reports having *felt* and *experienced* God at a deeper level. Her experience with God was accompanied by heightened awareness of all of her senses, and a deeper omnipresence than she had experienced in the natural world. Her smell, touch, sight, taste, and hearing could connect with God, and she used this *sensory language* to communicate with Him without verbal dialogue. Notably, McVea concedes that she did not witness a "human manifestation" of God. She did not see His hands, face or feet. She did not see a man with long, white hair, donning a tupa, and a flowing beard. Instead, McVea saw a radiant light. His presence, she says, while invisible to the eye, was *known*.

Perhaps the most profound thing about McVea's NDE is not the encounter itself, but what preceded it. Immediately prior to the experience, McVea, a mother of four, described her perception of God as cruel and authoritative. Her NDE gave her insight into what she describes as the "real" nature of Christianity, and allowed her to free herself from her perception that God was incapable of loving, and in particular, incapable of loving her.

McVea's also reports having received a message from God as doctors were frantically working to resuscitate her. She recalled wanting to move onto eternal life in Heaven and being very reluctant to come back to earthly consciousness. It was only when God asked her to convey her experiences to the natural world. "Tell them what you can remember," He said.

McVea, a private person with deep inner conflict, ultimately complied with the request from what she perceived to be God. Nervous about how people would perceive her account, she grappled with the request, fearing that her loved ones and others would dismiss her as delusional. Her internal struggles made her even more reluctant. Her physical abuse experienced during childhood and an elective abortion that she kept from her loved ones made her feel less deserving, and perhaps less accepting, of God's request. McVea recalls God perceiving her apprehension, and God's response. In her words, "When God gives you instructions, you have to comply." McVea's experience is described in greater detail in her memoir, "Waking Up In Heaven."[8]

---

[8] http://abcnews.go.com/blogs/health/2013/10/28/crystal-mcvea-claims-she-spoke-with-god-in-near-death-episode/

NDE Accounts – OBEs

One of the hallmarks of the NDE is the out-of-body experience (OBE). Conceptually, the OBE is simple, and exactly what the name suggests: *the experience of being, or viewing the world, outside of your body.*

Jazmyne Cidavia-DeRepentigny

Jazmyne Cidavia-DeRepentigny was lying still on an operating table. And suddenly, she wasn't.

Jazmyne floated over her body, levitating above what could have been a mirror. There were doctors. There were nurses and assistants. There were machines, and wires, and scrubs, and at the center of it all, there was Jazmyne. She saw herself as they saw her. *They were talking about her, but not with her.*

Jazmyne reports leaving the room before returning to the operating table to revisit herself. Upon seeing her body, she recalls immediately knowing not only that she was dead, but *how she died.* According to Jazmyne, her specific cause of death was asphyxia due to a defect in the breathing tube and too much anesthesia.

During her NDE, Jazmyne remembers trying to use her mind to move her right hand. She recalls seeing her hands extended parallel to her body and recoiling in terror when her efforts were unsuccessful. She tried desperately to move and pull the breathing tube out of her mouth, but to no avail. In the nadir of her despondency, Jazmyne looked down at her face and saw the inexplicable: one of the nurses blotting her own stray tears from her cheek.

According to her account, this prompted Jazmyne to try again. With her waning strength, she focused on whipping her now lead-heavy body into moving her hand until finally, she felt a flinch in the back of her palm. *Movement!* Her next memory was a flurry of clamor. Her tube was withdrawn from her throat, and an oxygen mask was drawn across her nose. *"Breathe,"* she thought, until she did.

Incredibly, the NDE at the operating table was not Jazmyne's first. She had an NDE experience when she was hospitalized at the age of thirteen. It would also not be her last.

Years later, Jazmyne had another OBE. During this third NDE, she describes seeing her "ghostly beautiful" entity clad in a white, free-flowing, loose gown standing before her. The apparition, standing approximately 6-8 feet from her body, wore a bright, soft halo. She recalls confusion while she stood watching what she perceived as her own "spirit" looking back at her limp, lifeless, color-drained body. According to Jazmyne, she could feel the calming warmth of her spirit's illuminating rays against her skin. After some time, the spirit then began moving away from her body. As Jazmyne and her spirit parted ways, the spirit waved goodbye to her physical body, then walked until it disappeared into a circular, luminescent opening in the air.

Like Crystal McVea, Jazmyne felt an inner conflict as her spirit moved towards the light. She remembers wanting to remain on earth, but also vividly recalls a strong "pull" beckoning her to follow her spirit into the light.[9]

Dr. Rajiv Parti

A fundamental misconception about NDEs is that they do not affect the rational. Many of us assume that since NDEs are not widely accepted as truth, scientists, medical practitioners, and skeptics must be immune to such occurrence. This assumption, of course, could not be further from the truth.

On December 24, 2010, Dr. Rajiv Parti, Chief of Anesthesiology at Bakersfield's Heart Hospital and founder of the Pain management institute of California, was rushed to the emergency room. According to the doctors, Parti presented with sepsis, a critical, and often fatal, infection. Prior to his admission to the emergency room, Parti had been from prostate cancer, along with a host of ancillary conditions arising from complications with his condition, including impotency, chronic pelvic pain, and incontinence.

Parti was admitted to the ER in a state of immense pain. During the acutest phases of his agony, Parti reports witnessing what he describes as his own "spirit body" floating 10 feet above his physical body. He could see doctors, nurses, and the medical team. He saw them working to save him.

Although Parti's account initially appears similar to other NDE accounts, including Jazmyne's, one critical distinction is that he reports not only leaving his

9 http://beforeitsnews.com/alternative/2014/05/my-spirit-told-my-body-goodbye-for-my-spirit-saw-the-light-and-wanted-to-go-into-it-jazmynes-near-death-experience-2965782.html

body, but leaving the immediate vicinity where his body resided. Specifically, Parti claims that during his OBE, he journeyed not only outside the operating room, but to *India*. Parti reports looking on as a casual observer as his extended family prepared a meal.

Parti also recalls a darker chapter of his NDE. According to Parti, after visiting his family in India, he traveled to a dimension he referred to as "hell," whereupon he began experiencing a "life review" and encountered deceased loved ones. In his next phase, Parti remembers walking through a tunnel and into what he believed to be Heaven. While there, he met what he describes as God, standing alongside two guardian angels. These "beings of light" assured Parti that he would be safe, and that upon returning to his physical body, he would leave his anesthesiology practice, forsake his materialistic life, and become a healer.

Upon returning to his conscious body, Parti claims that his psychological, mental and behavioral perspective shifted. In the weeks that followed, he ditched his career, moved from his 10,000 square-foot mansion and moved into what he described as a more modest home. He traded in his Mercedes and Hummer for a hybrid. Finally, he left his medical practice to start his new life performing volunteer work for community projects, where he counseled others on addiction, depression, chronic pain, and other "diseases of the soul."[10]

---

[10] http://www.laweekly.com/arts/dr-rajiv-partis-hellish-out-of-body-experience-changed-his-life-4448860

NDE Accounts – Ascension (Anonymous)

As indicated in the first chapter, while most NDEs accounts have consistent features, all NDEs manifest differently. One of the most compelling and unique NDEs was based on the account of an anonymous experiencer who reports an NDE that occurred thousands of miles above the earth's surface.

The anonymous experiencer describes himself as a 40-year-old male who was angry with everyone, including himself. He had two failed marriages that he admits destroying through his own verbal, physical, and emotional abuse. The experiencer provides details of his own infidelity in both marriages. The experiencer questions his own motives for remaining in the marriages at one point, and observed that love, to him, "was a complete waste of time and a show of weakness."

The experiencer's NDE account begins after an excursion in the desert. While driving his RV back home, he approached a busy intersection at a speed of 60 miles per hour. As he applied the brakes, he noticed that the RV was not slowing down. The brakes had failed. He downshifted gears to decelerate, but the RV continued plowing ahead, gaining speed with its momentum. A collision was imminent.

As he approached the intersection, he laid on the horn. The first vehicle approached. He quickly swerved out of the way, only to meet a second vehicle on the far side of his own vehicle. The RV was broadsided, went airborne, flipped on its side, and landed. Surely, this was the end.

The man recalls drifting in and out of consciousness while being transported to an ambulance and glancing down at his own blood-soaked clothes. The excruciating pain in his head was the effect of his skull being fractured in two locations. The waning sound of the intense discussion between doctors filtered through him as he faded toward the unconscious realm. Yet, there was no sudden darkness, and no immediate conclusion. On the contrary, his journey was just beginning.

He watched helplessly as his spirit vacated his body, until the eyes of the spirit became one with his own. He stared at his own lifeless body in all of its disrepair. He remembers the sight of his own blood engulfing his arms, legs, torso, and head. He recalls the pace of his ascension being slow and methodical. And then...speed.

He accelerated toward a celebration of colors, separate at first, then blending together as his pace intensified. The lights were before him, behind him, and on either side. The euphoria overwhelmed him as he soared, regretting only that he couldn't see fast enough to comprehend the majesty of his flight. At the apex of his speed, the beautiful array of luminescence congealed into a single, blinding white tunnel. As he was traveling through the light, he underwent a moment of complete catharsis. All the anger and hatred he had stored in his heart vacated, and with it, left all fear about his own fate.

He also reported losing the ability to communicate. He had no control over his ability to talk, with only his internal musings and sight at his disposal. Like others, he recalls physical transportation during his journey, as the light carried him to different "worlds," each with different colored skies. He witnessed different civilizations and life-forms. Some of them he thought were beautiful; others he described as frightening.

His account details how his understanding of his previous life varied and was vastly different from the life he was experiencing. "My thoughts kept going back to the beauty before me," reflected the experiencer, "and kept on implying that I must curtail my egotistical nature in the assumption of being the only intelligent being in the universe." Once he became aware of this ascension, his voyage came to an immediate stop. Next, an immediate loss of sight, and finally, a heightening of all other senses and emotions. According to the experiencer:

> In this instance, I was given insight into the future and shown that in a future not so far away, written and spoken word would cease to be a necessary form of communication....This realization brought with it a sudden stop in a plane or state of consciousness where I was surrounded by a blend of orange-golden light. In this plane, there existed varied spirits that were easy to identify and some that were difficult to identify....I was overcome by a feeling of unconditional love that was all-fulfilling and all around and within my being. This love was all

consuming, and in that moment, I desired nothing more than to remain there and experience this love for all of eternity.

The experiencer then reports an encounter with an omniscient "being":

In this instance, I felt the emanation of a highly evolved spirit heading towards me; his immense love, strength, and compassion engulf me. Telepathically, he gave me an account of my past lives and questioned me. I was compelled to answer truthfully because in my comprehension, I knew the being would know if I lied.

The being then informed me that the [purpose of] the experience was to show me that unconditional love was a beautiful and powerful force because its beauty was created by a benevolent creator.

The being went on to explain that war and suffering were creations of man, not man's creator, and that death was not a scourge, but rather a blessing:

Death is a gift from the creator, his greatest gift. Its purpose is to transition the spirit into the realm you're presently in and other higher realms. In this plane, the body you [formerly inhabited] would be destroyed by the unconditional love you're experiencing right now. Your spiritual fruition will manifest to alter your bodily form. Therefore, you must learn that the creator is benevolent. If it were not so, it would be impossible to live life after life until you learn your lesson.

The experiencer reports wanting to continue this discussion with the being, but the ascension had begun to end. He was overcome by a feeling that he was starting to slip away from the connection with the being:

At this instance, I started to ask a question but within, I felt something slipping.... [T]he swift passage sensation feeling overcome and regardless

of all my efforts, nothing I did could reverse the
process and return me to the beautiful realm.

After the ascension ended, the experiencer reports having regained his sight and seeing his spirit leisurely return to his body. His next recollection is the sound of voices from his doctors. Upon realizing that he had returned to the conscious plane, he was overwhelmed by great sadness and a feeling of loss. All the peace and love he had felt while in the other world dissipated and was displaced by his pre-ascension emotions of anger, hate, and aggression. The doctors, he recalled feeling, had violated his "right to passage" into the other life, and interfered with what he described as the "natural process."

What the experiencer didn't realize in that moment is that while he was in the other plane, he had "brought something back[11]."

---

[11] http://www.greatdreams.com/nde1.htm

NDE Accounts – Tracy Morgan

In 2014, a Walmart tractor-trailer collided with actor/comedian Tracy Morgan's limousine van on the New Jersey Turnpike, resulting in a six-car crash.[12,13] Morgan was rushed to the hospital with a broken leg and femur, broken nose, several broken ribs, and a life-threatening brain injury.[14] He spent 8-10 days in a coma, a period of time that he claimed, during an interview with Oprah Winfrey dramatically transformed his life. During his hospitalization, Morgan recalled ascending into heaven, where he met with his deceased father, Jimmy Morgan. Upon seeing his father, Morgan claims that his father, who was wearing "a green thing" during their encounter, told Morgan that heaven was "not ready" for Morgan. Morgan also recalled his emotional reaction to seeing his father again, telling Winfrey that he "started crying so hard, probably harder than" Morgan did at his father's funeral.[15] Morgan also claimed to have talked to God during his encounter.[16]

According to Morgan, the experience fundamentally changed him, but for the better. Once a person has been to the other side, Morgan opines, that person can never be "normal" again. Morgan believes that something is "different" in the way he interacts with others. He now finds himself saying "I love you" more often, even to those he does not know. According to Morgan, human beings are supposed to take care of one another, so rather than express concern over how his personality has changed, he welcomes it. He believes that he has "tapped into humanity and love," and that these new, overwhelming feelings of compassion

---

[12] "Tracy Morgan injured in car crash told to 'stay strong'," Chicago Tribune (June 7, 2014), available at: http://www.chicagotribune.com/news/chi-tracy-morgan-car-crash-20140607,0,1945423.story.

[13] Joe Sutton and Faith Karimi, "Actor Tracy Morgan in critical condition after six-vehicle accident in New Jersey," CNN (June 7, 2014), available at: http://www.cnn.com/2014/06/07/showbiz/tracy-morgan-hospitalized/index.html?hpt=hp_t1.

[14] "Tracy Morgan 'More Responsive' Day After Crash, Rep Says," ABC News (June 8, 2014), archived from the original on June 11, 2014, available at: http://abcnews.go.com/Entertainment/tracy-morgan-responsive-day-crash/story?id=24045450.

[15] http://www.supersoul.tv/supersoul-sunday/how-tracy-morgans-near-death-experience-changed-him.

[16] http://www.inquisitr.com/2597695/tracy-morgan-coma-talk-with-god-science-proves-near-death-experience-is-real/#47p2rqUBRdMLtyyv.99.

are fundamental to the human design. "We're supposed to take care of each other," Morgan tells Winfrey. "I'm not mad at nobody."[17]

The portion of the Winfrey interview devoted to Morgan's NDE was brief, but significant for two reasons. First, Morgan's visceral recollection of his father's green clothing is consistent with other accounts that reference vivid colors, including the anonymous "Ascension" account from the previous chapter. Green, in particular, is a color that has featured prominently in other NDE accounts. The "green thing" Morgan described his father wearing is remarkably similar to the "green tunic" worn by a doctor in one Ecuadorian woman's NDE account.[18] Jayne Smith, another notable experiencer, recalled in her account standing in "an absolutely beautiful green meadow," and described the "green of the meadow" as "fantastic."[19]

Second, Morgan's reference to a cathartic outpouring of grief is noteworthy. Other NDE reports describe "pain and sorrow,"[20] while still other experiencers recall feeling "amazing" and "at peace," with "all fear, anger, sadness, and negative emotions" removed.[21] While NDE accounts vary as to the type of emotional reactions elicited in the experiencer (from ecstasy to horror), Morgan's crying episode during his conversation with his father is nonetheless consistent with the intense emotional release prevalent among NDE accounts.

Morgan's experience may be what the NDE community has been lacking: a high-profile celebrity whose willingness to share an experience with the afterlife is part of a greater purpose, one that outweighs any potentially adverse effects to his professional reputation. Perhaps most encouraging for supporters of NDE awareness is Morgan's final comments about his experience, which suggest that the Oprah Winfrey interview may only be the beginning for Morgan's advocacy. "I went to the other side. This is not something I'm making up," Morgan said. "Do you know what God said to me? He said, 'Your room ain't ready. I still got

[17] http://www.supersoul.tv/supersoul-sunday/how-tracy-morgans-near-death-experience-changed-him.

[18] http://www.nderf.org/NDERF/NDE_Archives/NDERF_NDEs.htm.

[19] http://www.near-death.com/experiences/notable/jayne-smith.html.

[20] http://www.nderf.org/NDERF/NDE_Archives/NDERF_NDEs.htm.

[21] http://www.nderf.org/NDERF/NDE_Archives/NDERF_NDEs.htm.

something for you to do.' And here I am, doing an interview with [Oprah Winfrey]."[22]

Morgan does not offer any details about his mission during the Winfrey interview, but does reveal two critical components: (1) his NDE was the inspiration for it; and (2) the Winfrey interview was the initial step in fulfilling it. Regardless of whether or not you believe his account, Tracy Morgan believes that he traveled to the afterlife and returned with a divine mandate to promote humanity and love among all inhabitants of the living world. While reasonable minds can disagree as to the credibility of his inspiration, when an influential social icon sets out to achieve such selfless objectives, can the living world afford to dismiss him?

---

[22] http://www.inquisitr.com/2597695/tracy-morgan-coma-talk-with-god-science-proves-near-death-experience-is-real/#47p2rqUBRdMLtyyv.99.

Conclusion

What will *you* see before you die? Will you see the pearly gates of Heaven, as Crystal McVea did? Will you stealthily levitate above your doctors like Jazmyne Cidavia-DeRepentigny, or will you travel to your fatherland, as Dr. Parti did? Will you see a single white light, or will there be a brilliant spectrum of colored rays? Will you reunite with your late father, or have the chance to chat with God, as Tracy Morgan did? Or will you have your own unique experience, and will you get the chance to live again to tell about it?

Science indicates that NDEs are mere psychological and physiological occurrences that can be explained. While we live in a world driven by logic and reason, some things cannot be explained by rational concepts. The NDE experience is a profound experience that fundamentally alters the experiencer's life.

Importantly, while the individual accounts of experiencers may differ, there are a number of parallels common to most NDE accounts: (1) the out of body experience; (2) immense, blinding, and intoxicating light; (3) travelling through a tunnel and into another plane; (4) encountering God and/or conversing with being of light and/or a deceased loved one; and (5) a deep sense of change after the experience.

There's no doubt that science has added immense value to our humanly lives, but we must also comprehend that the beauty of science cannot explain everything we perceive. Can 40% of the human race be liars? Can they all be hallucinating or mentally disturbed? There's only way to find out.

Preview: Understanding the NDE Through Meditation

A special gift for you

Dear Reader:

Thank you for your business! I hope you enjoyed this brief primer on NDEs, and that you now have a better understanding of what is waiting for you at the next stage of your journey. For more information about my mission and projects, or if you'd like to reach out to me directly, please feel free to visit me at my author page.[23]

You made this book possible. As a special thank-you for your support, I have included below a FREE preview of the next installment in this series: Understanding the Near Death Experience Through Meditation.[24] I wish you the best of luck in your journey toward understanding, enlightenment, and truth. Farewell for now, and never stop learning.

-Thad

...

Joni Maggi described herself as agnostic – she didn't believe in God, but she also didn't *not* believe in God. In the early 1980s, after having recently separated from her husband, Maggi was living with her four-year-old son in South America. She recalls being in a state of "emotional crisis," living with depression and a feeling of utter loneliness. One day, Maggi sat down to meditate. What happened next, chronicled in Kevin Williams' critically-acclaimed book, *Nothing Better Than Death: Insights From 62 Profound Near-Death Experiences*,[25] would forever change her core beliefs about life, death, and all that lies in between:

[23] https://www.amazon.com/-/e/B01BR05N62.

[24] http://amzn.to/2l7Z6Rt.

[25] Williams, K. R. (2002). *Nothing Better Than Death: Insights From 62 Profound Near-Death Experiences,* 33-35. Xlibris, *available at* http://amzn.to/2l8zuGO.

Close your eyes for a moment and try to imagine that you are face to face with the sun! What an extraordinary feeling! I thought to myself: "How can I be face to face with the sun and not feel the burning heat?" It was literally so bright that I could not sustain the gaze so I turned away. At that moment I noticed a silver cord, attached around the navel area going down, down, down to a person I saw lying on my bed. It was me! I had a curious non-interest in it. Suddenly, I was in dark outer space, floating as it were on my back, in what I can only describe as total "bliss" (one of a few words which I'll explain later I had never understood before that point!)....I then looked down and could see the Earth - far far away and down in this dark sky. I knew that it was a place of violence, a realm shrouded in darkness and difficulties, so to speak.

In this excerpt, Maggi encounters a bright light, whose brilliance she compares to the sun, but without the extreme heat. In addition to the experience with a bright light, which, as discussed in Chapter 2, regularly appears in the accounts of NDEs, Maggi also provides a detailed description of the separation from her own body, consistent with the "detachment" hallmark shared between meditation and NDEs. Perhaps most significant about this particular element of Maggi's NDLE, and in contrast to the many OBE-NDE accounts, is that Maggi's detachment was not complete: she retained her physical connection to her earthly body via a "silver cord" attached at the navel. Maggi's "detachment by attachment" in her dance with the afterlife bears an obvious parallel to the pre-life stage of human gestation. In Maggi's NDLE, her desire to progress down life's next challenge is tempered by the need for security and attachment. The silver cord attached to her navel ensures she is at all times united with the known quantity that is her corporeal body, a need that mirrors the pre-life connection to the familiarity of the womb by way of the umbilical cord.

In addition to detachment, Maggi's NDLE featured an elevated sense of consciousness and awareness:

...This first thought shocked and puzzled me - to be thinking in the way I would normally think....I'm not sure how long this ecstatic feeling lasted but it was what I suppose is called Cosmic

Consciousness or cosmic bliss. ...What happens is that you let go of daily consciousness and slip into another. Or for that matter, like waking up - you let go of sleeping consciousness and find yourself in our recognized reality.

Maggi's heightened consciousness in the NDLE has two layers of significance. The first layer, her achievement of a state of altered and heightened consciousness, is a fundamental and expected symptom common to meditation-induced NDLEs. The second layer, which is far more unique, is her ability to recall her awareness of her own self-bewilderment – or the *awareness of heightened awareness* – that adds intrigue to her account. The capacity for self-reference, to detail the experience within the experience, is what makes Maggi's NDLE not only uniquely valuable to the field of near-death studies, but also comforting to those who treasure the gift of human rational thought and hope to retain it throughout the afterlife.

Finally, Maggi's account contains multiple references to the third shared hallmark between meditation and NDEs, clarity:

It was an incredible feeling of peace to know that there is no death!...I knew that: the Universe is upheld by love (though if you ask me now I would not be able to explain that!)...I knew that the planets are alive and conscious. I knew that they would never bump into each other on purpose or cause any damage - there was no violence but rather a total harmony in their existence....

The word choice in the passage above is especially interesting, not only for those that were chosen, but for those that were not. Maggi wasn't describing an emotion or any other subjective concept. She doesn't talk about a "feeling" that death didn't exist, she didn't say that she "thought" the universe was upheld by love, or even that she "believed" that the planets enjoyed a harmonious coexistence. Her refrain was simple, unequivocal, and above all, clear: she "*knew*" those things. They were true:

I have spent the last 20 years, trying to recapture...that absolute knowing....I also know that it was real! Actually, I could say that it was the only real thing that has ever happened to me.... And again

28

> *I knew - or understood in an instant that death is exactly like falling asleep*

But the parallels between Maggi's NDLE and the traditional NDE don't end with the three shared hallmarks (clarity, detachment, consciousness). Other features common to NDEs also appeared in Maggi's NDLE, including an encounter with beings of light:

> *At one point I saw what I can only describe as a group of beings - perhaps Beings of Light would describe them best. I then zoomed over to them - literally willed myself over to them (swoosh!) and was there instantaneously. They were seated...in an oval circle and there seemed to be a leader of some sort at the head of the group.*

> *First of all, I felt the most overwhelming love coming from them! It cannot be compared to anything here on Earth. For one, I felt that it was an inclusive group - rather than an exclusive one. (Here on Earth we seem to have trouble letting new people into groups but there it was as if all of them at the same time were welcoming me!) I heard them - in my mind - say, "Welcome home! You have been on such a long journey!" I had the feeling that they were sharing life experiences and learning from each other, as if in a sort of classroom.*

Maggi's NDLE also featured a realization that she had a moral obligation to return to the physical world and raise her son:

> *...[A]t this point I said to the leader, again, telepathically, "I cannot stay! I have to bring up my son!" with a real sense of urgency....At the time my son was 4 years old and I knew somehow that I had the absolute obligation to bring him up and take care of him. Years later, when I thought of this, I understood that we live in a "moral" Universe.*

For reference, below are the NDE hallmarks we identified in Chapter 2:

1. Ineffability
2. Notice of Death

3. Tranquility and Comfort
4. Out-of-Body Experience
5. The Dark Tunnel
6. Interaction
7. Beings of Light
8. Life Review
9. Unusual Sounds
10. The Border
11. Reluctant Return

Recall that some of the more remarkable accounts from Dr. Raymond Moody's study from *Life After Life*, including the one analyzed in Chapter 2, presented with only three of the 11 hallmarks. Maggi's experience featured four: Tranquility and Comfort, Out-of-Body Experience, Beings of Light, and Reluctant Return.

Upon leaving her spiritual journey, Maggi, like many other NDE experiencers, returned to the physical world with a redefined sense of purpose, but with an excitement tempered by the sobriety that accompanies a lack of support from loved ones:

> *This is the first time I am sharing my experience so openly with others because my family and friends, of course, at the time did not believe me or understand me....Now, it is probably the most important thing I can do - to remember it and to share it with others. If it hadn't been for the experience[,] I probably would not have pursued the spiritual path with such relentless passion as I understand that there is a spiritual need which cannot be filled by any other thing than ... how shall I call it? The "spirit."...And it has only whetted my appetite to know more - everything! - about our life purposes, life after death, etc!*

As Maggi returned from her NDLE, she received parting advice from her new friends from the afterlife:

> *I immediately started coming down again. And as I was coming down, I saw - as if written on the entire dark sky - this message: "There is nothing worth worrying about! Not even death!"*

Joni Maggi's NDLE is not simply significant from an academic perspective. It's a reminder to all of us that death, while inherently no more kind than life, is not an ominous enterprise. As such, life and death should more appropriately be viewed as two sides of the same coin: while the two concepts are different, neither is bad nor good, nor better or worse, than the other. Perhaps Maggi explains it best:

> Death is like falling asleep or like waking up. We leave one state of consciousness and enter another.

...

To continue reading, purchase *Understanding the Near Death Experience Through Meditation* **today.**[26]

---

[26] http://amzn.to/2l7Z6Rt.

Suggestions for Further Learning

Thank you again for purchasing this book! I hope you have a better understanding of the near death experience, and I wish you the best of luck in your journey toward understanding, enlightenment, and truth. If you enjoyed this book, please be so kind as to leave a review on Amazon at http://amzn.to/2jj4ksV!

Below are a few suggestions for furthering your learning in the field of near-death studies:

Proof of Heaven: A Neurosurgeon's Journey into the Afterlife: http://amzn.to/2ig5moo

Life After Life: The Bestselling Original Investigation That Revealed "Near-Death Experiences": http://amzn.to/2jvs8t7

Understanding Life after Death: http://amzn.to/2ijCCOu

Near Death in the ICU: Stories from Patients Near Death and Why We Should Listen to Them: http://amzn.to/2gcjaAm

Near Death Experiences of Doctors and Scientists: Doctors, and Scientists Describe Their Personal Near-Death Experiences: http://amzn.to/2g8hxT6

Hereafter: http://amzn.to/2fie9rl

Flatliners: http://amzn.to/2g8hVAZ

Farewell for now, and never stop learning.